HOW DO CATERPILLARS BECOME BUTTERFLIES?

DARICE BAILER

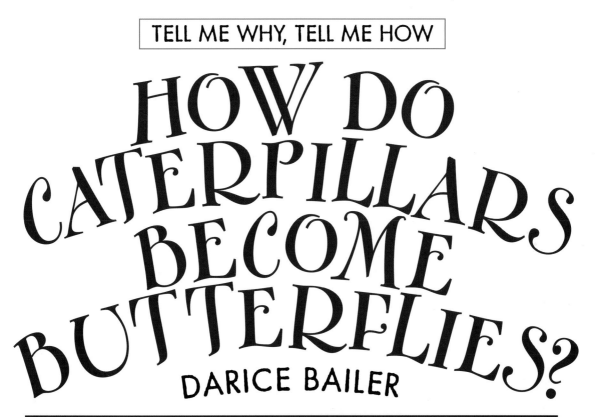

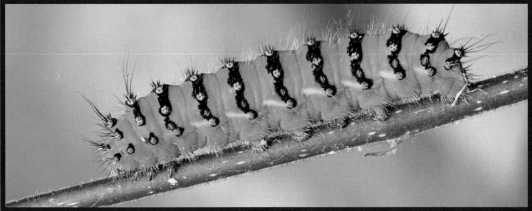

Marshall Cavendish
Benchmark

New York

Marshall Cavendish Benchmark
99 White Plains Rd.
Tarrytown, NY 10591-5502
www.marshallcavendish.us

All websites were available and accurate when this book was sent to press.

Library of Congress Cataloging-in-Publication Data
Bailer, Darice.
How do caterpillars become butterflies? / by Darice Bailer.
p. cm. — (Tell me why, tell me how)
Includes index.
Summary: "Provides comprehensive information on the process of
caterpillars changing into butterflies"—Provided by publisher.
ISBN 978-0-7614-3987-5
1. Butterflies—Life cycles—Juvenile literature. I. Title.

QL544.2.B34 2009
595.78'139—dc22

2008019732

Photo research by Candlepants Incorporated.

Cover Photo: Jim Brandenburg / Minden Pictures

The photographs in this book are used by permission and through the courtesy of:
Corbis: Herbert Zettl/zefa, 1, 5; Fritz Rauschenbach/zefa, 7; Ralph A. Clevenger, 8; Robert Pickett, 9; Frans Lanting, 12. Minden Pictures: Jef Meul, 3; Tim Fitzharris, 13; Frans Lanting, 19, 18; Thomas Marent, 20; Michael and Patricia Fogden, 23; Kim Taylor, 24. Photo Researchers Inc.: Charles W. Mann, 6. Shutterstock: 10; 22. Getty Images: Charles Krebs, 14; Garry Gay, 15; George Grall/National Geographic, 25; Craig Tuttle, 16. Super Stock: age fotostock, 21.

Editor: Joy Bean
Publisher: Michelle Bisson
Art Director: Anahid Hamparian
Series Designer: Alex Ferrari

Printed in Malaysia

1 3 5 6 4 2

CONTENTS

What Is a Butterfly? – 5

The Four Stages of Butterflies – 9

Growing Inside a Shell – 13

The Butterfly Appears – 19

Life as an Adult – 23

Activity – 27

Glossary – 29

Find Out More – 31

Index – 32

Butterflies start their lives
as caterpillars.

What Is a Butterfly?

Butterflies are some of the prettiest insects in the world. Each one has colorful wings that carry it gently to flowers on a sunny day.

Yet butterflies begin life looking very different. They start out as eggs that hatch into . . . caterpillars! A caterpillar is the eating and growing stage of a butterfly's life.

Butterflies belong to the same group of insects as moths. Both female butterflies and female moths lay eggs that hatch into caterpillars. The caterpillars eat and grow for about two weeks and then go through a **metamorphosis**. That means a complete change in shape or looks.

This caterpillar has been eating and growing. It is getting ready to change into a butterfly.

The caterpillars that come from moth eggs turn into moths inside a silk case called a cocoon. The caterpillars from butterfly eggs become butterflies inside a hard shell, or **chrysalis**. Butterflies are usually more colorful than moths, and they have knobs on the ends of their **antennae**. Moth antennae are straight or feathery.

Butterflies first appeared when dinosaurs roamed the earth, 65 million to 135 million years ago. Today they are found everywhere in the world except the North Pole and the

This caterpillar is called a woolly bear because of all its hair. One day it will become an Isabella tiger moth.

continent of Antarctica. Butterflies cannot live in those areas that are cold because they are cold-blooded. They need the heat of the sun to warm themselves.

Butterflies also need the sun in order to fly. The average butterfly cannot fly when the temperature is below 60 degrees Fahrenheit (15.5 degrees Celsius). It can walk around, but it does not move around too much. Butterflies sometimes look dead until the sun warms them up again.

This butterfly has warmed its wings in the sun and is now flying to a flower.

Where does the word *butterfly* come from? No one knows for sure. It might come from a butterfly in England known as the yellow brimstone. This butterfly is the color of butter, and it was known as the butter-colored fly.

All butterflies go through four stages during their lives. They begin life as an egg. Here you can see the next three stages: caterpillar, pupa, and emerging butterfly.

The Four Stages of Butterflies

Butterflies go through four stages during their lives: egg, caterpillar, **pupa**, and butterfly.

Butterfly eggs are tiny and have thin shells. The shells are also hard, so they protect the baby caterpillars inside.

Once they hatch, baby caterpillars are very picky eaters. They eat just one or two kinds of plants. Caterpillars will eat all day long after they hatch—but they would rather starve than eat something they do not like!

The female butterfly knows that her offspring will be picky. She looks around for just the right plant for her babies. When she sees one, she tastes the plant with the pads of

A caterpillar hatches and crawls out of its eggshell.

her feet to be sure. When the mama butterfly finds a plant her caterpillars will like, she lays her eggs.

About three to seven days later, the eggs darken, and the first caterpillar eats its way out of its shell. This caterpillar, which is also called a **larva**, has very sharp jaws that can grind leaves to bits.

The caterpillar's jobs are to eat and to grow. After all, it needs energy for the next stage, when it changes into a butterfly. The caterpillar's skin cannot grow or expand as it eats, though. It outgrows its skin the way you grow out of your clothes. Soon the caterpillar's skin feels too tight, and it grows a new skin underneath the top one.

A monarch caterpillar hangs upside down after gluing itself to a twig. Then it curls up, sheds its skin, and forms a hard shell.

The caterpillar then curves its body, bursts open the skin on its back, and **molts**. It wiggles headfirst right out of its old skin! The old skin is now a dry husk, and the caterpillar takes off in its new, larger skin.

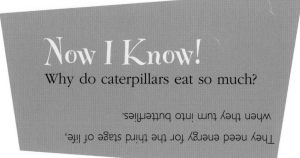

Now I Know!

Why do caterpillars eat so much?

They need energy for the third stage of life, when they turn into butterflies.

Caterpillars molt four or five times as they grow. They can eat their weight in food several times a day. In fact, they grow to 27,000 times their size at birth!

Finally, about two weeks after hatching, the caterpillar has eaten enough. Now, the caterpillar squirts out silk threads from a tube on its lower lip called a **spinneret**. The sticky threads clump to form a strong button, and another strand becomes a belt. The caterpillar grabs the silk button with its hind legs, glues itself upside down, and hangs from its belt.

The caterpillar molts one last time. It sheds its skin as well as its head, mouth, and legs! The new, soft skin hardens into a chrysalis. The well-fed caterpillar will never look the same.

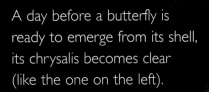

A day before a butterfly is
ready to emerge from its shell,
its chrysalis becomes clear
(like the one on the left).

Growing Inside a Shell

It takes one to two weeks for the caterpillar to change into a butterfly inside its chrysalis. The caterpillar has stomach juices to break down all the leaves it ate. Now these juices turn its old body to mush.

Like other insects, butterflies have a head, a **thorax** (chest), and an **abdomen** (tail end). They have two antennae attached to their head above their eyes. Butterflies also have two pairs of wings.

Caterpillars have six eyes on each side of their heads. Their eyes can tell light from

Butterflies have two antennae, which they use to smell things.

dark, but they cannot see objects clearly. Butterflies need sharper eyes so that they can see in every direction. This way, the butterflies can escape from **predators** and find food or a mate. A caterpillar's twelve little eyes turn into two **compound eyes**. There are six thousand tiny lenses in each eye.

This image shows an extreme close-up of a butterfly eye.

Caterpillars crawl, but butterflies are able to fly. The butterfly keeps the caterpillar's three pairs of front legs. These legs are hinged, so they are good for landing and walking. The caterpillar's back legs disappear, though. They make way for four large wings.

A new pair of long, knobby antennae helps the butterfly smell its food. The new butterfly does not chew plant leaves like a caterpillar because it does not have a mouth or jaws. Instead, the butterfly sucks up **nectar**, a

Butterflies suck up nectar, the sweet juice made by flowers.

sugary liquid inside flowers. The butterfly also drinks the juices of rotting fruit, tree sap, bird **dung**, and water.

A butterfly eats with a long, curly tongue called a **proboscis**. This tongue is like a drinking straw that the butterfly uncurls and sticks into flowers or rotting fruit. The

Butterflies do not chew their food like caterpillars. They drink their food with a long, curly tongue.

butterfly then sucks up sugary liquids through this straw.

Like magic, the old chewing mouth of the caterpillar disappears, and a curly proboscis grows in its place. The butterfly will be able to coil up its proboscis when it is not eating.

As the birth of the butterfly nears, the chrysalis darkens. Colors are appearing on the wings of the butterfly. They appear through what is now a clear shell.

Now I Know!

When do caterpillars become butterflies?

In the third stage of life, while they are inside a chrysalis.

A monarch butterfly is
fully formed and is
now breaking out of its
chrysalis. Soon it will
hang free and rest.

The Butterfly Appears

When a butterfly becomes fully formed, its body swells against the walls of the chrysalis. The wall splits, and the butterfly crawls out headfirst. Its brand-new wings are now crumpled and wet.

Butterflies first **emerge** in the morning. They are **diurnal** insects, which means they are active during the day. Birds and lizards—the predators of butterflies—are not as active during the day, so the new butterfly has a better chance to survive.

A butterfly rests on the shell of its chrysalis. It dries its new wings before flying for the first time.

After coming out of the chrysalis, the butterfly rests for one to three hours. Its abdomen is swollen with blood, and it pumps blood through veins into its wings. Soon, the wings are full-size, and the butterfly is finished growing. Females are usually born larger than males so that they can carry eggs.

As the butterfly waits for its wings to dry and harden, it has another job to do. Its proboscis looks like two black threads. The butterfly coils and uncoils its proboscis until the threads fuse into a drinking tube.

The wings on this brand-new butterfly are reaching their full size. Soon the butterfly will fly off and leave its chrysalis behind.

A close-up look at a butterfly's proboscis.

Soon the butterfly's wings are rigid and strong. It spreads its wings, opening and closing them to try them out. Then the butterfly flutters off. Though it is a bit wobbly, it is able to make its first flight.

Two red-spotted purple butterflies meet on a flower to mate.

Life as an Adult

The caterpillar's job was to eat and grow. Now, the butterfly's job is to find a mate and to lay eggs for new baby caterpillars. Female butterflies are attracted to a male's smell or the color of his wings. When butterflies find a partner, they mate on the ground, on a plant, or in the air. They fly off alone when they are done.

The female then hunts for a safe place to lay her eggs, away from birds and lizards. A monarch butterfly lays

A pierid butterfly lays her eggs on a leaf. She knows that her caterpillars will like to eat this plant once they hatch.

between one hundred and four hundred eggs, either on top or under leaves. Most butterflies lay just one egg at a time. Some lay a bunch of eggs at once. Some butterflies lay as many as 1,300 eggs before they die.

The female butterfly does not stay to watch over her eggs. Instead, she flies away and leaves them alone.

Butterflies live anywhere between two days and a year, depending on what type they are. The average butterfly lives just two weeks.

Some butterflies can survive the winter, when temperatures freeze and food disappears. When icy winds blow, the mourning cloak butterfly hibernates. It takes cover

A group of butterfly eggs are gathered underneath a leaf. Here they are hidden from predators.

These monarch butterflies are stopping to rest during their migration.

inside a hollow tree or under a piece of bark. Its body contains chemicals that keep it from freezing to death. During the wintertime, its body nearly shuts down.

Some butterflies **migrate**, or move, to get away from the cold. Monarch butterflies are born throughout North America. They also live in South America, the Caribbean, Australia, and New Zealand. Monarch butterflies that are born at the

Now I Know!

How long does the average butterfly live?

For two weeks.

end of summer in North America fly to California, Florida, or Mexico for the winter. They can fly up to 100 miles (160 kilometers) a day and total more than 2,000 miles (3,200 km) as they go where their great-grandparents once traveled. There, thousands of monarchs huddle on trees in bright orange and brown clusters. When spring comes, they return north to lay their eggs.

Then they will die, and baby caterpillars will be born. New life begins.

 Activity

You can observe a caterpillar eat, grow, molt into its chrysalis, and emerge as a gorgeous butterfly.

The best way to raise butterflies is to buy their favorite flowers and plant them in your garden. Butterflies enjoy black-eyed Susans, purple coneflowers, asters, zinnias, marigolds, and sunflowers, among others. You can easily grow some of these plants from seed. Do not use any pesticides to kill garden pests, as the poison will kill the butterflies, too!

To raise a butterfly, follow these steps:

1. Capture a caterpillar on its leaf and gather fresh leaves from the same plant. Remember, caterpillars will starve to death rather than eat food they do not like! Collect a few sticks and a piece of bark, too.

2. Find a clear jar or container. Place a wet piece of paper towel on the bottom, and cover it with fresh

leaves. (Make sure they are leaves from the plant where you found your caterpillar!) Place a cover on the container.

3. Keep your caterpillar away from direct sunlight, where it might get too hot.

4. Clean your caterpillar's home each day. Do not touch the caterpillar, though. Throw away the old leaves and replace them with fresh ones. Put the new leaves on top of a clean, wet paper towel. You can leave the caterpillar on its original leaf.

5. If your caterpillar looks like it is sleeping, do not bother it! It may be ready to climb to the top of your cage, molt for the last time, and form its chrysalis. Then, about one to two weeks later, you are in for an amazing treat—the metamorphosis of your caterpillar into a butterfly!

6. After your butterfly emerges and its wings have had a chance to harden, take it outside in its container. Open up the container and place it near some flowers so that your butterfly can fly out and eat a good meal!

 Glossary

abdomen—The tail end of an insect.

antennae—The sensing organ on the head of an insect.

chrysalis—Another name for a butterfly pupa. It is shaped like a teardrop and often has gold highlights. The word *chrysalis* comes from the Greek word *khrusos*, meaning "gold."

compound eyes—Eyes that are made up of thousands of tiny eyes that enable an animal to see in all directions at once.

diurnal—Active during the day.

dung—Solid animal waste.

emerge—To come out or appear.

larva—The second stage of a butterfly's life; a caterpillar.

metamorphosis—A major change in form or shape.

migrate—To move from one country or region to another.

molts—Sheds one's outer skin.

nectar—A sugary liquid inside flowers.

predators—Animals that hunt other animals for food.

proboscis—A thin, hollow tube through which a butterfly drinks.

pupa—The third stage in a butterfly's life, when it changes from a caterpillar to a butterfly inside a chrysalis.

spinneret—A tube on a caterpillar's lower lip that holds the glands that make silk.

thorax—The middle section of an insect's body.

Find Out More

BOOKS

Berger, Melvin and Gilda. *Butterflies & Caterpillars: Scholastic True or False*. New York: Scholastic, 2008.

Cussen, Sarah. *Those Beautiful Butterflies*. Sarasota, Fla.: Pineapple Press. 2008.

Heiligman, Deborah. *From Caterpillar to Butterfly Big Book*. New York: HarperTrophy. 2008.

Kant, Tanya. *How a Caterpillar Grows into a Butterfly*. New York: Children's Press, 2008.

Slade, Suzanne B. *From Caterpillar to Butterfly: Following the Life Cycle*. Mankato, Minn.: Picture Window Books. 2008.

WEB SITES

Discover photos and facts about butterflies
www.backyardnature.net/buttrfly.htm

Help track monarch butterflies on their annual journey to Mexico and back
www.learner.org/jnorth/monarch/index.html

Learn more about caterpillars and butterflies
www.butterflyschool.org

Index

Page numbers in **boldface** are illustrations.

abdomens, 13, 20
antennae, 6, 13, **13,** 15

birds, 19, 23
butterflies, **4,** 5–7, **18, 22, 23, 25,**
  25–26
  emerging, **8, 18, 19,** 19–20
  females, 5, 9–10, 20, 23–24
  stages of life, 5, **8,** 9–11

caterpillars, **5,** 5–6, **6, 8, 9,** 9–11
chrysalises, 6, 11, **12,** 13, 17, **18,** 19,
  19, 20, **20**
cocoons, 6

diurnal insects, 19

eggs, 6, 9, 20, **24**
  laying, 5, 10, **23,** 23–24, 26
eyes, 13–14, **14**

flying, 7, **7,** 15, 21, 26
food, 9, 13, 14, 15–17, **23**

heads, 13
hibernating, 24–25

Isabella tiger moths, **6**

larvae, 10
legs, 15

lizards, 19, 23

mating, **22,** 23
metamorphosis, 5, 11, 13–15, 17
migrating, 25–26
molting, 11
monarch butterflies, **18, 25,**
  25–26
monarch caterpillars, **10**
moths, 5–6
mourning cloak butterflies, 24–25

nectar, **15,** 15–16, 17

pierid butterflies, **23**
predators, 14, 19, 23
proboscises, 16, **16,** 17, 20, **21**
pupae, **8,** 9

red-spotted purple butterflies, **22**

spinnerets, 11
sun, the, 7

thoraxes, 13

wings, 5, 13, 17, **19,** 20, **20,** 21,
  23
woolly bear caterpillars, **6**

yellow brimstone butterflies, 7